Mother Teresa

Mother Teresa

A Pictoral Biography

JOANNA HURLEY

An Imprint of Running Press
Philadelphia • London

A Running Press Book

© 1997 by Michael Friedman Publishing Group, Inc.

All rights reserved under the Pan-American and International Copyright Conventions.
Published in the United States in 1997
by Courage Books, an imprint of
Running Press Book Publishers.

Printed in Hong Kong

10 9 8 7 6 5 4 3 2 1

Digit on the right indicates the number of this printing

ISBN 0-7624-0214-8

MOTHER TERESA
was prepared and produced by
Michael Friedman Publishing Group, Inc.
15 West 26th Street
New York, New York 10010

Editor: Stephen Slaybaugh
Art Director: Jeff Batzli
Designer: Andrea Karman
Photography Editor: Karen Barr
Production Manager: Camille Lee

Published by Courage Books, an imprint of
Running Press Book Publishers
125 South Twenty-second Street
Philadelphia, Pennsylvania 19103-4399

ACKNOWLEDGMENTS

Thanks to pacifist writer Virginia Olsen Baron, whose path in the pursuit of worldwide
peace crossed Mother Teresa's in Kathmandu, where she gained the insight that helped me see Mother Teresa more
clearly; and to my editors, Sharyn Rosart and Stephen Slaybaugh, who helped me shape this book.

DEDICATION

Like Mother Teresa herself, this book is dedicated to hungry children
everywhere; may the day come soon when they hunger no more.

Contents

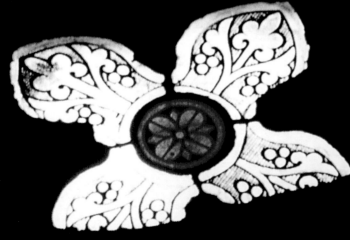

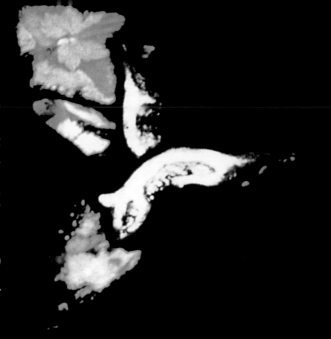

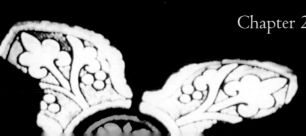

Child of the Balkans, Citizen of the World

Her face is recognized across the

globe: Mother Teresa of Calcutta,

the Nobel Prize laureate, the nun

in a sari—to many, a living saint.

When she began to feed the

poor of India in 1946, it was with

her own hands, often with food she

WORLD-FAMOUS FOR CARING FOR THE POOR, MOTHER TERESA HAS OFTEN REMINDED THE
WORLD THAT SHE IS A NUN, NOT A SOCIAL WORKER, AND THAT PRAYER AND COMMUNICATION
WITH GOD IS AT THE DEEPEST HEART OF HER EVERY ACT.

begged for on the streets of Calcutta; when she retired fifty-one years later, it was as the founding

head of a four-thousand-strong order of nuns, with houses in virtually every nation. Perhaps never

before in history has a woman become so famous so far from the place—and circumstances—of

her birth.

From the heart of the war-torn Balkans, the bloodiest site of European nationalism, Agnes

Gonxha Bojaxhiu became the living renunciation of nationalism: a citizen of India and an apostle

CHILDREN ARE CLOSE TO THE CENTER OF MOTHER TERESA'S MISSION. IN 1946, WHEN SHE

HEARD A CALL TO LEAVE THE CONVENT AND LIVE AND WORK AMONG THE POOR OF CALCUTTA,

SHE BEGAN BY TEACHING THE POOREST OF THE CHILDREN AND WENT ON TO FEED

THE HUNGRIEST AMONG THEM.

MOTHER TERESA'S WORK HAS TAKEN HER ALL OVER THE WORLD. HERE SHE IS ESCORTED TO
SHORE AFTER ARRIVING IN WAR-TORN LEBANON FROM CYPRUS.

of love beyond borders. Born at the dawn of the profound changes of the twentieth century, she

took on a centuries-old garb—and life. Vowed to poverty and humility, she has met with four popes,

and has been honored by innumerable kings, queens, and heads of state. She has been pictured on

the covers of numerous magazines throughout the world. She has also been criticized for imposing

her own doctrines on the poor of other cultures than her own.

Mother Teresa's own explanation of her extraordinary story is that it was God's plan, that

she was merely an instrument of divine will. But the details—and the single-minded passion—that

were the engine of that plan were her own, as are the responses to the criticisms leveled at her.

This is one account of those details and that passion.

PART I
BEGINNINGS
(1900-1928)

Chapter 1

THE BALKANS

IN THE FIRST DECADE OF THE TWENTIETH

CENTURY, A PHARMACIST NAMED NICOLA

BOJAXHIU AND HIS YOUNG WIFE,

DRANAFILE, LEFT THEIR HOME OF

SHKODRA IN NORTHERN ALBANIA.

THEY MOVED PERHAPS A HUN-

DRED MILES TO THE SMALL CITY OF

MOTHER TERESA HAS ALWAYS FOCUSED ON CHILDREN. HERE SHE MEETS SOME YOUNG
GIRLS IN MANILA.

Skopje. The move was and wasn't an emigration. Skopje lies well outside Albania, in the Kossovo region of what is now Macedonia in Serbia. But it was then, as it is today, populated primarily by Albanians. At the time, both Albania and the Kossovo region were within the Ottoman Empire, and Nicola and Dranafile were merely moving from one part of the empire to another.

The agony of the Balkans is no modern development. On the contrary, it extends back for four millennia into the dawn of European history, far beyond the Bosnian and Serbian struggles that have been the tinderboxes of the twentieth century.

The 250,000-square-mile triangle that is the Balkans runs south from central Europe to the Mediterranean. Its rugged mountain passes—*Balkan* is Turkish for "mountain"—form a major land route between Europe and Asia. It has been a battleground since at least 2000 B.C., when the

RUSSIA

AUSTRIA-HUNGARY

BOSNIA

Sarajevo •
HERZEGOVINA

SERBIA

ROMANIA

Bucharest •

MONTENEGRO

BULGARIA

Sofia •

Skopje •

BLACK
SEA

Monastir
(Bitola) •

THRACE

Constantinople •

ITALY

Salonika
(Thessalónika) •

ALBANIA

MACEDONIA

Corfu

GREECE

OTTOMAN
EMPIRE

AEGEAN
SEA

Athens •

IONIAN
SEA

Crete

Boundary of the Ottoman Empire in 1912
before the Balkan Wars

//// Territory lost by the Ottoman Empire
during the Balkan Wars, 1912-1913

Hellenic peoples began to fight their way from the north into the sunny peninsula on the Mediterranean. Ever since, the Balkans—settled, resettled, and fought over by dozens of peoples—have been the scene of Europe's fiercest nationalist struggles. These conflicts carved out the nations of Albania, Bulgaria, Greece, the European portion of Turkey, Slovenia, Croatia, Bosnia and Herzegovina, Yugoslavia, Macedonia, and Romania.

In the years before World War I, much of the tension in the Balkans emerged from a regional desire for independence from the Turks. In 1911, Bulgaria, Serbia, Greece, and Montenegro joined together as the Balkan League to attempt to pry Macedonia out of the moribund Ottoman Empire. Then, in 1912 and 1913, as western Europe prepared to face off against the Turks and the decaying Austro-Hungarian Empire, two smaller—some think, preparatory—wars broke out in the heart of the Balkans. Between them, they wrested Albania and Macedonia from the Ottomans, though Macedonia's independence turned out to be brief.

In 1914, a gunshot elsewhere in the Balkans, in Sarajevo, where the Archduke Francis Ferdinand of Austria-Hungary was assassinated by a Serbian nationalist, precipitated the first World War. In 1918, when the Great War was over, Albania retained its independence, but Macedonia was incorporated into the new nation of Yugoslavia, which also comprised Serbia, Montenegro, and parts of the old Austro-Hungarian Empire.

Through those turbulent years, Nicola and Dranafile (she was called *"Drone,"* Albanian for "rose") Bojaxhiu lived at the center of the nationalist struggle over Albania and Macedonia. The Ottomans had Islamicized those parts of the Balkans under their control, but the Bojaxhius were part of the Catholic Albanian (and Macedonian) minority.

To complicate matters further, Nicola was an Albanian nationalist. Skopje was not far from Albania, and, in the words of one biographer, the Bojaxhius "felt and spoke Albanian." During and after the war, Nicola was active in the effort to make Kossovo a part of the newly independent Albania.

Instead, Macedonia—including Kossovo—became part of Yugoslavia. In time, Nicola's opposition would cost him and his family dearly.

Agnes' Childhood

When Nicola and Drone arrived in

Skopje, Nicola was as interested in

taking care of his growing family

as he was in Balkan politics.

He was much older than

Drone when they married—at age

thirty-four, he had lived more than

MOTHER TERESA'S MISSIONARIES OF CHARITY NOW HAVE HOUSES IN DOZENS OF COUNTRIES
AROUND THE GLOBE, MANY OF THEM DEVOTED TO CHILDREN WHO HAVE BEEN ORPHANED OR ABANDONED.
HERE MOTHER TERESA BEAMS HER TRIUMPH AT OPENING YET ANOTHER, THIS ONE IN HONG KONG.

twice her sixteen years. In Skopje, instead of practicing as a pharmacist, Nicola went into con-
struction. Business prospered and so did the family. Their first child, a son they named Lazar, was
born in 1908; Drone was not yet eighteen years old. Two years later—on August 26 or 27, 1910
(accounts vary)—Drone gave birth to the daughter who would become Mother Teresa. They chris-
tened her Agnes but called her *Gonxha*, Albanian for "[rose]bud." In 1913, they had their third and
last child, a second daughter, named Age, or Agatha.

The two major sources of information about Agnes' early years contradict each other at points. Mother Teresa herself has spoken little about her childhood; her few statements tend to refer glowingly to a "joyful" and "united" family that was pious and peaceful. Her father, she has said, was an upright man who gave unstintingly to the poor and who spoke fluent Albanian, Turkish, and Serbo-Croatian, a necessity in that turbulent region. Drone, whom Mother Teresa refers to as the soul of the family, was passionately devout.

But when Mother Teresa received the Nobel Prize for Peace in 1979, her brother Lazar, the only other surviving Bojaxhiu, conveyed to a few journalists a darker picture of their childhood. Nicola's ceaseless advocacy for an Albanian Kossovo, he said, earned him the enmity of the Yugoslavian authorities that shadowed their lives.

Otherwise, the family life described by both Lazar and Mother Teresa was a happy one. Their home was spacious, with a garden that held a small guest house. The Catholic chapel was nearby, and Drone and her children attended mass every morning. The children started school at the church as well. There they were taught in the Albanian language, but when the new nation of Yugoslavia instituted compulsory public education, the schools taught in Serbo-Croatian. (Serbo-Croatian is one language written in two alphabets: Croatian in Roman letters, Serbian in Cyrillic.)

Even as a child, young Agnes was principled and religious. She never tattled on her sister and brother when they did forbidden things such as filching extra portions of sweets, but she herself would never join them. Even then, Lazar has said, she seemed to have a special affinity for the poor. Drone visited the poor regularly; Lazar and Agatha avoided accompanying her as much as they could, but Agnes went willingly: "There was a poor widow who lived with her seven children in a dark and dirty room....Agnes was almost always there with those dirty and malnourished children."

And so they might have gone on—contented, prosperous, and unremarkable—had tragedy not struck the family the year Agnes turned nine years old.

Chapter 3

Nicola's Death

In the early years of Mother Teresa's fame, when she was asked about her family, she told interviewers—and reportedly even her own spiritual adviser—only that her father had died suddenly in 1919, when he was forty-six years

THE SHOCK OF HER FATHER'S EARLY DEATH MAY HAVE CONTRIBUTED TO THE FUTURE NUN'S
ENDURING AFFINITY FOR ORPHANS; HERE SHE IS AT THE ORPHANAGE IN CALCUTTA WHERE SHE
BEGAN CARING FOR CHILDREN WHO HAD LOST THEIR HOMES AND FAMILIES.

old. Her mother, Mother Teresa said, had been so devastated by his death that she had fallen into a deep depression, unable to leave the house for months.

Then, impelled by necessity—the family no longer had a source of income—Drone roused herself and went into business selling embroidered fabric from their home. She must have been an extraordinary woman, for the Bojaxhius were soon able to live as well as they had when Nicola was still alive.

Sixty years later, long after Drone and Agatha had died, Lazar added several crucial details to the account of Nicola's death: it was 1919. The Great War was over, Yugoslavia was a nation, and Nicola—by that time a member of the Skopje city council—and other Albanian nationals in the new nation agitated for Kossovo to be incorporated into Albania.

AS SOON AS MOTHER TERESA SECURED PERMISSION FROM THE CHURCH TO OPEN MISSIONS OF CHARITY OUTSIDE INDIA, SHE GRAVITATED TOWARD WAR-RAVAGED CITIES AND COUNTRIES. MOTHER TERESA TALKS WITH THE INDIAN AMBASSADOR TO LEBANON AND HIS WIFE IN BEIRUT IN 1982.

His stance was not a popular one with the new Yugoslav government. They harassed Nicola continually, said Lazar. Sometime that year, Nicola traveled to Belgrade for a meeting, presumably a political one. He came home terribly ill, suffering from severe abdominal pains; eventually, he was admitted to the local hospital. He died there soon afterward, poisoned, Lazar affirmed, by the Yugoslav police, who had him "eliminated for political reasons." (The death certificate, however, made no mention of poison.)

Mother Teresa has never confirmed nor denied Lazar's account. Her authorized biography, published after the death of all the principals in the story, is silent as to a possible cause of her father's death.

Chapter 4

OCATION

IN 1922, WHEN AGNES WAS TWELVE

YEARS OLD, SHE HEARD A PAIR OF

JESUIT MISSIONARIES FROM INDIA

PREACH IN SKOPJE. THEY GAVE, SHE

SAID LATER, "SUCH BEAUTIFUL

DESCRIPTIONS ABOUT THE EXPERIENCES

THEY HAD WITH THE PEOPLE, AND

WHATEVER AGNES ENVISIONED AS A CHILD WHEN JESUIT MISSIONARIES FIRST CAPTURED HER IMAGINATION, SURELY PLAYING HOST TO POPES, ROYALTY, AND PRESIDENTS WAS NOT PART OF THE PICTURE. HERE SHE MEETS WITH POPE JOHN PAUL II.

especially the children, in India." It was then that she felt her first clear impulse to work with the poor; the picture that came to her was specifically of India.

There was only one problem: "[She] did not want to become a nun." She was, after all, a girl at the beginning of adolescence. Nevertheless, Agnes shared her idea with her mother. Devout as she was, Drone didn't leap at the idea. Instead, she told Agnes that she was much too young to think about such things. Perhaps, too, Drone was reluctant to part with Agnes. The family had recovered—to the extent it ever would—from the shock of Nicola's death, but surely Drone depended on her responsible, serious older daughter.

So Agnes put the idea aside and went on about her business, which consisted of school on the one hand and her church's youth group on the other. A good student, she began teaching in a small way; through the church, she gave religious instruction to younger children. The teaching experiences were deeply rewarding to her, but all the while, her attention was caught, over and over, by the stories she heard in the church group of the missionaries, most especially those about India.

MOTHER TERESA HAS TAKEN MANY JOURNEYS IN HER LIFE.

HERE SHE VISITS SISTERS IN OSLO, NORWAY.

Then, through the church group, she learned of a group that would take on increasing importance to her: there was a three-century-old order of nuns—the Sisters of Loreto—based in Ireland that sent nuns to teach in India.

Six years after Agnes felt those first stirrings of a great calling, the question came to a head. It was 1928, and Agnes was about to turn eighteen. One day, reading some letters from Jesuits in India, she experienced a moment of clarity regarding her future. She had realized some time back that teaching—and working with the poor—comprised a kind of vocation for her. Now, in one moment, her reluctance to take the veil evaporated. She knew, as clearly as she had ever known anything, that she would become a nun and go to India. Years later, describing that life-changing moment to a biographer, she pointed upward and said, "He made the choice."

Her decision must have come as something of a shock to Drone, for when Agnes told her, Drone went into her room and stayed there for twenty-four hours. When she came out, Drone was reconciled to Agnes's choice.

As soon as she had told Drone, Agnes went to her priest to discuss her decision. When he told her that a true vocation for the religious life was always accompanied by feelings of intense joy, she knew she had made the right decision.

In an orderly and businesslike way, Drone and her daughter investigated how best for Agnes to pursue her vocation. In the end, they hit on the very order Agnes had heard about years before, the Sisters of Loreto, which trained nuns to teach in India. Before going to India, however, Agnes would have to travel to the Sisters of Loreto's mother house in Ireland to train in nursing and to learn English.

On September 28, 1928, a month after turning eighteen, Agnes, Drone, and Agatha boarded a train in Skopje. They were going to Zagreb together, where they would say good-bye.

A few days later, Agnes boarded another train in Zagreb, this time heading west out of Yugoslavia on the first leg of the long trip to Ireland. She took that train by herself, leaving her sister and mother behind in Zagreb. She never saw Drone—or her sister and brother, or Skopje—again.

Part II
The Nun
(1928-1946)

Chapter 5

AGNES CHANGES HER NAME

AGNES (AS SHE STILL WAS CALLED)

STUDIED AT THE SISTERS OF LORETO

CONVENT IN RATHFARHAN, NEAR

DUBLIN, FOR A MERE TWO MONTHS. ON

NOVEMBER 28, 1928, SHE LEFT

IRELAND, EMBARKING ON A SEVEN-WEEK

INDIA WAS IN A TUMULTUOUS STATE WHEN AGNES ARRIVED; MOHANDAS GANDHI WAS
BEGINNING TO LEAD HIS COUNTRY TO FREEDOM. JAILED REPEATEDLY BY THE BRITISH,
HE NEVER LOST FAITH IN NONVIOLENCE AS THE ONLY PATH.

journey to Calcutta. The young nun traveled first by sea to Bombay, then overland across India. She

arrived in Calcutta in January 1929.

India was in turmoil—a turmoil that must have been all too familiar to the young nun from

the Balkans. The British Raj still ruled there, but more tenuously with each passing year. In 1929,

millions rallied to the cause of independence, via either the nonviolent, largely Hindu movement

represented by the India Congress Party led by Mohandas K. Gandhi and Jawaharlal Nehru, or the

Muslim League of Mohammed Ali Jinnah.

Only two years earlier, the appointment of an all-British commission to "investigate" the question of India's government had sparked riots throughout the country, and the British had capitalized on the opportunity to jail Gandhi.

At nineteen years of age, Agnes did not yet identify herself as Indian. By the time of India's independence seventeen years later, she was ready to take Indian citizenship. In spite of the echoes of her childhood resounding in the struggle around her, at that time she remained aloof from Indian politics. She was, after all, a nun—not even a nun yet but a postulant.

From Calcutta she made her way to Darjeeling, the hill city to the north, where the British administrators summered and where the Sisters of Loreto convent was located. One of the nuns who served at the convent at the time remembers Agnes as a "simple, ordinary girl."

Later that year, the order gave Agnes her first assignment: to go back to Calcutta, live at the Sisters of Loreto convent in the Entally neighborhood, and teach geography at St. Mary's High School for Girls. The assignment would turn out to be the last she ever received; she remained at St. Mary's for seventeen years, until a second "call" led her to leave the convent and found her own.

On January 24, 1931, Agnes took her preliminary vows as a Sister of Loreto. The name she chose was Sister Teresa—not, as is often said, for the great Spanish mystic St. Teresa of Avila but for the "little" Teresa, St. Thérèse of Lisieux. Inspired by the simple goodness of her namesake, the path of Sister Teresa's life seemed set clearly in front of her: for the rest of her life, she would live the life of a teaching nun in the shelter of the convent.

It was a comfortable occupation for the young nun. She loved the religious life: the discipline, the prayers, the society of her peers. She was a good teacher; as the women she taught as girls in Calcutta say, she made geography—and the Catechism—"come alive."

Yet all along, the poverty she saw firsthand haunted her. Later, she would say that she "[felt] it very deeply that (while) I should be snug in my bed...down the road there (were) those who have no cover."

On May 24, 1934, at the convent in Darjeeling, she took her final vows. She was twenty-three years old.

JUST BEFORE INDEPENDENCE: THE LEADERSHIP OF THE ALL INDIA CONGRESS, THE PARTY OF
GANDHI (SEATED, CENTER) AND JAWAHALARL NEHRU (SEATED, IN CHAIR), WHO BECAME THE
NEW NATION'S FIRST PRIME MINISTER.

The Humblest of Saints: Thérèse of Lisieux (1873-1896)

Along with her vows, Agnes Bojaxhiu, who had been called *"Gonxha,"* or "Rosebud," at home, took a new name as a nun in 1931. She called herself Sister Teresa, after the French Carmelite nun Thérèse of Lisieux, the "Little Flower of Jesus."

St. Thérèse had been canonized only six years earlier, a mere twenty-eight years after her death of tuberculosis in 1896 at the age of twenty-four. In her short life she had become the apotheosis of humility; so moved was her mother superior by the frail young nun's spirituality that she asked her to write her autobiography. When Thérèse was canonized, it was as the saint of "the little way."

Born Marie-Françoise Thérèse Martin in Bordeaux in 1874, she was the seventh daughter and ninth and last child of Louis Martin, a soldier, and his wife, Marie Azélie, a lacemaker. Of the Martins' five daughters who survived infancy, four would eventually become nuns in the same Carmelite convent, including Thérèse, the youngest. But none of her sisters would bring to the religious life quite the same passion as did Thérèse.

It was a passion formed by a unique combination of joy and sorrow. After Thérèse's birth, the family moved to the

MOTHER TERESA IDENTIFIED STRONGLY WITH THE "LITTLE" THÉRÈSE, THE CARMELITE NUN WHOSE FRAIL HEALTH—SHE DIED AT 24—FORCED HER TO FIND SANCTITY IN THE SMALLEST ACTS OF DEVOTION.

town of Alençon, famous for its laces. But Marie Azélie—called Zélie in the family—was already in her forties and may have already been suffering from the breast cancer that would kill her four years later. Unable to nurse her baby, she was forced to send the child to a wet nurse in the next town, five miles away.

The Martin family was middle-class and educated; Zélie's two oldest daughters, Marie and Pauline, were away in boarding school when Thérèse was born. Our knowledge of the saint's childhood is due primarily to extant letters between Zélie and her older daughters.

Zélie was overjoyed when little Thérèse returned home in the spring of her second year; she was, wrote the proud mother, a "big baby, tanned by the sun." By Thérèse's own account, the next three years were happy ones for the baby of the family; idolized by her father, she was indulged by everyone. She was robust and a touch mischievous, although even at that tender age, she showed an unusual interest in all things pertaining to God and religion. At the age of two and a half, she told Zélie, "I wish you would die, dear little mother, because I want you to go to heaven."

It was a wish that was to be fulfilled all too soon. Thérèse's happy life changed drastically when Zélie died of breast cancer in 1877. The family moved to nearby Lisieux to be near a brother of Zélie's. So stunned and grief-stricken was the little girl by the move and the loss of her beloved mother that her outgoing personality disappeared, replaced by such acute shyness that Thérèse was unable to attend school and had to be educated at home. Her only comfort was the presence of her older sister Pauline, who had returned home and who became Thérèse's "second mother."

But at nine, Thérèse lost her second mother when Pauline became the first of the daughters to join the Carmelite convent at Lisieux. This second loss was devastating to Thérèse, who became ill, possibly with the onset of tuberculosis. She remained unwell for much of the next several years. Five years later, in 1886, the next sister, Marie, entered the same convent. It was a third dreadful loss for the now thirteen-year-old

Thérèse; it would become a turning point in her life.

That year, when the family celebrated Christmas, Thérèse prayed for relief from the feelings of bitterness that possessed her. It was then, she later wrote, that charity entered her soul: suddenly, all she wanted was "to love Jesus with a passion." She decided that she, too, would become a nun.

It was not easy to convince her father to let his youngest daughter go, but she did it; perhaps she knew, even then, that she had little time. It turned out, however, that Louis was not to be the highest hurdle between her and her new, burning desire. The local Catholic hierarchy was opposed to the idea of permitting so young a child take the serious step of entering the religious life.

To console her, Louis took the remaining family on a trip to Rome. There they arranged an audience with Pope Leo XIII. The rules were that the Pope might speak to his visitors, but they were forbidden to speak to him; in what would be a last breach of humility for Thérèse, she nevertheless burst out, "Holy Father, let me enter the convent."

The Pope was not about to put aside all the rules for an unruly fourteen-year-old, but her plea or her prayers must have moved someone. When the Martins returned home, the Bishop of Lisieux relented, and Thérèse was permitted to join her sisters the next year, at the age of fifteen.

Thérèse had one more disappointment in store; safe at last inside the convent, she was not permitted, because of her physical frailty, to use any of the tra-

ditional means—such as fasting—to attain greater closeness with God. It was then that she began the spiritual journey that would make her a saint. "I wanted to seek out a means of going to heaven by a little way," she wrote. The answer that came to her was from the Bible: "Whoever is a little one, let him come to me." She understood that she must become childlike, that instead of attempting to find sanctity, she only had to "trust Jesus like a father." Instead of great sufferings, she would give herself wholly to every small task that came her way.

She became more proficient in humility than any nun had ever been before—so much so that the head of her order asked her to write out the story of her spiritual path. She had written two-thirds of the document when it finally became clear in 1896—she was then twenty-three—that she was very seriously ill. By then, she was hemorrhaging frequently; she was barely able to finish the book—called, in English, *The Story of a Soul*—before she died on September 30, 1897. Her last words were, "My God, I love you."

When Pope Pius XI canonized her in 1925, it was because she had "democratized" holiness. Today, September 30 is her feast day, and Lisieux, where she lived and died, is a major place of pilgrimage for Catholics.

STORM CLOUDS

IN 1934, THE SAME YEAR SISTER

TERESA TOOK HER FINAL VOWS IN INDIA,

HER MOTHER, SISTER, AND BROTHER

LEFT SKOPJE FOR GOOD AND RETURNED

TO THEIR HOMELAND OF ALBANIA. THE

THREE SETTLED IN TIRANA, THE CAPITAL

MOTHER TERESA BIDS HER SISTERS GOODBYE AS SHE DEPARTS FOR CYCLONE-DEVASTATED
AREAS OF SOUTHEAST INDIA.

It was a move that would ultimately prove to have far-reaching consequences, both to them and to the young nun in Calcutta.

Nothing untoward happened for the first few years; the family appears to have done well enough in Tirana until the outbreak of World War II five years later.

Their Agnes in Calcutta was also doing well; in 1937 Sister Teresa, only twenty-seven years old, became the principal of St. Mary's. With the new position came a new title. Despite her youth, she was now known by the honorific that has since then become familiar to the whole world: at the age of twenty-seven, Agnes "Sister Teresa" Bojaxhiu became "Mother Teresa."

But with the coming of the war, all their lives would change. In 1939, under Mussolini's fascist government, Italy invaded Albania. Lazar, then thirty-one, was "incorporated" into the Italian army and transported to Turin. It was another terrible loss for Drone; she never saw her son again.

Lazar spent the rest of the war in Italy. When it ended, he could have returned to Tirana but for one small problem: Albanians who had fought for Italy, however reluctantly, were not welcome there.

More than unwelcome, they were considered criminals. Eventually, under the postwar communist government of Enver Hoxha, a resistance fighter against the Italians during the war, Albania took action against the "traitors." Lazar was tried in absentia, found guilty, and sentenced to death.

As Lazar was in Italy, the sentence was never carried out. He remained there after the war, managing a pharmaceutical company. Drone and Agatha in Tirana were all that remained of the once-happy Bojaxhiu family of Skopje.

Chapter 7

WAR!

THOUGH THERE WAS MINIMAL FIGHTING

IN INDIA DURING WORLD WAR II, THE

COUNTRY NEVERTHELESS UNDERWENT

TERRIBLE AGONIES. WHEN THE WAR

BEGAN, THE JAPANESE HAD QUICKLY INVAD-

ED AND OCCUPIED THE NEIGHBORING

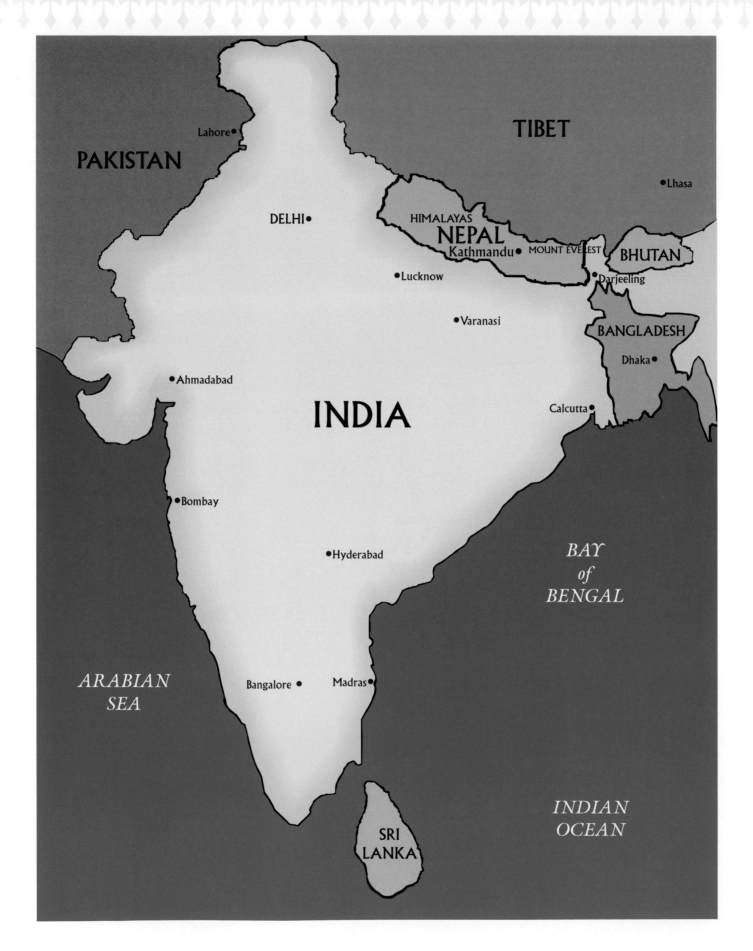

country of Burma, and there was every reason to think they intended to mount a full-scale invasion of India.

For Mother Teresa, gone was the calm of the cloister. As the center of the entire British operations in the East, Calcutta was subject to the constant threat of air raids by Japanese planes. There were, in fact, only a few such raids, but the fear was pervasive.

There were more mundane disruptions as well. In 1942, the British commandeered the Sisters of Loreto's Entally complex for administrative purposes, and the convent and school were forced to move to another location nearby.

Worse was to come. It had never been easy to deliver food to the teeming millions in India's cities, but the war caused the already-strained transportation system to deteriorate into chaos. In 1942, famine struck: the Great Famine, as it came to be called, lasted well into 1943 and claimed as many as two million lives.

Yet in the midst of the horror, Mother Teresa maintained some semblance of her nun's routine, managing to center each day on the two activities that were central to her life: teaching and prayer.

In 1944, she even found time to create a new, profoundly significant relationship. She met a Jesuit priest who would become one of the most important figures in her life, Father Celeste van Exem. Almost immediately, she claimed him as her spiritual adviser.

She would need his advice badly two years later when a thunderbolt struck in the form of a second call from Above.

Mohandas Gandhi and Indian Independence

Of all the independence struggles of the twentieth century, India's may be the most dramatic and the one with the most far-reaching consequences. Certainly its leader, the revered apostle of nonviolence Mohandas K. Gandhi—the *Mahatma*, or "Great Soul," as he was called in India—is one of the pivotal figures of the era. A profoundly gentle man imbued with deep Hindu mysticism, Gandhi nevertheless utterly rejected those aspects of Indian culture that divided his people—by religion or caste—embracing instead the tenets of democracy and equality. A man of the spirit, he was nevertheless a shrewd politician, with an uncannily accurate grasp of what tactics would work at what moment; a nationalist, he nevertheless rejected the notion that independence was worth killing for, though he was always ready to die for it, as, in the end, he did.

The British Raj ruled India when Gandhi was born into a high-caste family near Bombay in 1869. When he was nine years old, the British Parliament declared India an empire and Queen Victoria its empress. Gandhi was not taught rebellion at home; he married at thirteen, a normal event in his milieu. Leaving India at nineteen to study law in England ran counter to custom, however, and when he attended the University College in London, he encountered the forces that would shape his life: British racial prejudice, on the one hand, and, on the other, the principles of nonviolent resistance articulated by the nineteenth-century American philosopher Henry David Thoreau.

Upon receiving his law degree, Gandhi returned to India to practice, but soon moved to South Africa, also part of the Empire at the time. Although he was the first "colored" person ever permitted to practice before the country's supreme court, South Africa's rigid system of racial stratification intensified his resistance to discrimination of all kinds. In 1894, at the age of twenty-five, he took his first steps as a political leader by organizing the Natal Indian Congress to advocate for Indian rights in South Africa.

Not yet convinced that the liberation of the Indian citizens of the Empire would require the radical step of Indian independence, Gandhi organized an ambulance corps for the British during the Boer War (1899-1902). But in 1906 he began what would become a lifetime's work of nonviolent civil disobedience.

He declared that he would go to prison—or die—before he obeyed South Africa's anti-Indian laws. Deliberately, he set about to flout the laws; thousands of South African Indians joined him. He was sent to prison; it would turn out to be the first time of many.

In 1914, Gandhi returned to India, and in 1919 became one of the leaders of a new party, the Indian National Congress. The next year, he brought to India the ideas he had ripened in South Africa, urging the entire nation to spin its own cotton and to boycott all things British. He was imprisoned again; he had only recently been released when the young nun Agnes Bojaxhiu arrived in India. In 1930 he launched perhaps his most famous campaign, leading thousands on a two-hundred-mile march to the sea to make salt from sea water. Yet again, he went to prison.

By now Gandhi thoroughly believed that there would be no freedom for Indians as long as they lived under British dominion. At the advent of World War II the Indian National Congress offered Britain an ultimatum: India would help the Allies resist Japan in Asia if Britain would grant India its independence. For his part in the Congress' work, the government imprisoned Gandhi for most of the duration of the war. But the struggle with England was over: India—and Gandhi—had won. Britain ceded its dominion over the subcontinent in 1947.

The conflict within the country was only beginning, however. For a decade, Indian Muslims, under the leadership of Mohammed Ali Jinnah of the Muslim League, agitated for a two-state solution to the Indian question, and even Gandhi could not reconcile Muslim and Hindu India. Against Gandhi's opposition, the British Parliament's Indian Independence Act of 1947 created two states, India for the Hindus, under the government of Gandhi's close colleague Jawaharlal Nehru, and a two-part Pakistan—half of it northwest of India, half of it northeast—for the Muslims.

Unfortunately, this solution did not bring peace. Mass riots broke out all over India, killing tens of thousands. The riots were quelled only when Gandhi, then seventy-eight years old, set out to fast—if necessary, to the death—unless Muslims and Hindus made peace. Not until he was very near dying did the violence subside.

At least as much the father of his country as Washington was of the United States, Gandhi was by then so widely beloved that hundreds followed him every time he left his house. Yet not all Indians had been satisfied by the partition of India, and extremists on both sides bitterly resented his peacemaking. On 30 January 1948, Gandhi was assassinated by a Hindu extremist.

Though the nation was grief-stricken, and Gandhi widely venerated in it, his shining example never brought a permanent peace to his strife-ridden nation. Sectarian violence continued to take thousands of lives in India over the ensuing decades. In 1983 the Indian government under Prime Minister Indira Gandhi (not related to Mohandas, but the daughter of his colleague and India's first Prime Minister, Jawaharlal Nehru) ordered Indian

WITH INDIA STILL TORN BETWEEN RELIGIOUS GROUPS—BY THE 1980s, IT WAS SIKH VS. HINDU—MOTHER TERESA PRAYS FOR PEACE AT A MEMORIAL TO GANDHI.

troops into the holiest shrine of the Indian Sikhs, the Golden Temple in the Punjab; four hundred Sikhs died. A year later, Sikh guards assassinated Indira Gandhi.

Nor was the division of the one-time Indian Empire ended with the 1948 partition into India and Pakistan. The two widely separated halves of Pakistan never meshed comfortably into one nation, and after years of civil strife, East Pakistan declared its independence as Bangladesh in 1973.

But the legacy of Mohandas K. Gandhi was nonetheless far-flung and profound. On the one hand, he had

been a major force in the post-war ebbing of European political domination of Asia and Africa. On the other, his principles of nonviolent resistance and their success in India inspired a broader range of liberation struggles, not the least of them the U.S. civil rights movement that arose only a few years after Gandhi's death. In 1964 that movement's most famous leader, the Reverend Martin Luther King Jr. (who would four years later die as Gandhi had, at the hands of an assassin), won the Nobel Peace Prize for his nonviolent leadership, which had been directly patterned after Gandhi's.

Turmoil in India

Finally, in 1945, peace brought a dramatically changed world order. Japan was in ruins, ravaged by the fighting and by the final blow of the atomic bombings of Hiroshima and Nagasaki. The British were among the victors, yet their empire,

THE WARTIME FAMINE HAD DEEPENED MOTHER TERESA'S AWARENESS OF INDIA'S TERRIBLE
POVERTY...

too, was in tatters. India was not yet to know peace; it would become independent, divided into the
two nations of Pakistan and India.

But independence, once secured, did not come without cost. Food remained scarce; at St.
Mary's, Mother Teresa wondered how she would feed two hundred starving children.

With the 1946 partition into India and Pakistan, the disorder mounted. Six million people moved, some from India to Pakistan, some in the opposite direction. Hundreds of thousands of
people passed through Calcutta. Shanty towns sprung up all over the city. In August 1946, tensions
between Hindus and Muslims sparked rioting in the streets of Calcutta. Inadequate food supplies
only exacerbated the situation.

AND MAY HAVE HELPED OPEN HER HEART TO THE "CALL" SHE WAS ABOUT TO HEAR ORDERING
HER TO LIVE AND WORK AMONG THE POOR.

Yet in the midst of cataclysm, Mother Teresa had to maintain not only a school but her own

spiritual life. In September, she was scheduled to go to Darjeeling for a religious retreat. On

September 10, she boarded a train in Calcutta.

The train ride from Skopje to Zagreb in 1928 had seemed momentous to her, taking her,

as she thought then, across a border between one life and another. It was that journey, in a sense,

that had made a nun of her. The trip from Calcutta to Darjeeling in 1946 would, however, eventu-

ally make her world famous.

Chapter 9

THE SECOND CALLING

IT IS THE MOST OFTEN TOLD STORY OF

MOTHER TERESA'S LIFE. SITTING ON THE

CALCUTTA-TO-DARJEELING TRAIN, PRE-

PARING HERSELF FOR HER RETREAT, THE

THIRTY-SIX-YEAR-OLD NUN THOUGHT

ABOUT ALL THE THINGS SHE HAD SEEN:

THE WAR, THE TERRIBLE INTERNECINE

ON HER TRAIN RIDE ACROSS THE INDIAN COUNTRYSIDE MOTHER TERESA RECEIVED HER
SECOND CALLING.

strife, and the poverty. Most of all, she pondered the poverty: the hungry children of India, and the

people living and dying on the streets.

And as clearly as if someone were speaking from the adjacent seat, she heard what she later

referred to as an "order." She was to leave the convent and live and work among the poor.

"[God]," she has said many times, "wanted me to be poor and to love Him in the distress-

ing disguise of the poorest of the poor."

FROM THE WINDOW OF THE TRAIN BETWEEN CALCUTTA AND DARJEELING, MOTHER TERESA SAW
SCENE AFTER SCENE OF DESPERATE HUNGER AND PRIVATION.

Instantly she saw that following that order would not be easy. She was a nun, not an independent woman. She could not leave the convent without the permission of her superiors—it would possibly require the permission of an archbishop or even the pope.

Not for a moment did she contemplate leaving without that permission. She was, she believed, a bride of Christ, indissolubly wedded to Jesus; divorce was, literally, unthinkable. Nor, had she been able to contemplate it, would she have wanted it. Mother Teresa still loved her Bridegroom; her relationship with Him was the central fact of her life. It acted as her support, her food and drink, even the air she breathed.

No, if she were to obey this call—and failing to obey it was equally unthinkable—she would have to have that permission. All right, she thought. She would get it. If God wanted her in the streets of Calcutta, God would put her there.

And God would tell her what to do when she got there, that she knew. God would have to because, there on the train, Mother Teresa couldn't begin to think concretely about exactly what it was she would do or how she would live.

There was one more sense in which this move would not be easy, for she loved the convent life. Leaving it was "the most difficult thing I have ever done. It was a greater sacrifice than to leave my family and country to become a nun," Mother Teresa has said.

However, none of those things made her hesitate. The call was that clear.

IT BECAME CLEAR TO MOTHER TERESA THAT HER WORK FROM NOW ON WOULD BE TO DIRECTLY ALLEVIATE THE PEOPLE'S SUFFERING.

IN CALCUTTA, MOTHER TERESA SHOWS HIS HIGHNESS THE PRINCE OF WALES THE FOOD SHE
GIVES THE POOR OF HER ADOPTED CITY.

Part III
The Missionaries of Charity
(1946-1965)

Chapter 10

To Leave the Convent

These days, of course, the whole world recognizes the Nobel Prize laureate nun-in-a-sari who hob-nobs with popes and heads of state. But in 1946, Mother Teresa was just an ordinary nun, and no one who knew her had any reason to

GOD "WANTED ME TO LOVE HIM IN THE DISTRESSING DISGUISE OF THE POOREST OF THE POOR."

believe she would be chosen for such an extraordinary mission. She was asking for what the church calls exclaustration, the right to live and work as a nun outside the convent walls and associated with no order. Rare for any member of the clergy, in 1946 it was unheard of for a nun.

It took Mother Teresa two long years to get the permission she sought—or, rather, permissions: that of the head of her order, that of the archbishop of her diocese, and, finally, that of the pope himself. The first potential hurdle, however, was deceptively simple. Father van Exem, her own spiritual adviser, recognized at once the authenticity of her vision. He believed then, and believes still, that it came directly from God.

Archbishop Perier of Calcutta was less credulous. In one biographer's words, "the idea of a lone European nun on Calcutta's streets at a time of political and communal strife filled him with

"THE MESSAGE WAS CLEAR—I KNEW WHERE I BELONGED, BUT I DID NOT KNOW HOW
TO GET THERE."

alarm." Instead of working on her request, he had her transferred to the town of Asansol, northwest of Calcutta by about one hundred seventy-five miles. Nothing in her order from God had sug-
gested that she was to be excused from her vow of obedience, and Mother Teresa went to Asansol
and waited patiently. Finally, late in 1947, Archbishop Perier permitted her to write to Mother
General Gertrude of the Sisters of Loreto in Ireland.

Mother General Gertrude's response was immediate and in stark contrast to the archbishop's. She gave her wholehearted permission for Mother Teresa to ask for the final seal of approval
for her exclaustration—that of the Vatican. In July 1948, the word came from the pope: approved.
Mother Teresa would become the first Catholic nun in three hundred years allowed to work outside
a convent.

OUTSIDE THE WALLS

IT WAS A TURNING POINT IN MORE WAYS THAN ONE. NOT ONLY WAS MOTHER TERESA ABOUT TO DO SOMETHING REVOLUTIONARY IN THE WORLD, BUT THE PACE OF HER LIFE WAS ABOUT TO CHANGE PROFOUNDLY AS WELL.

MOTHER TERESA SHARING A MOMENT OF MERRIMENT WITH THE YOUNG NUNS OF THE
MISSIONARIES OF CHARITY.

It had taken her, for example, six years from her first stirrings of interest in missionary work to
decide to become a nun. Having decided, she had come to India and spent seventeen years teaching
there, nearly two of them waiting for permission to begin her new life. Now, however, things began
to move with astonishing rapidity.

Mother Teresa was feeling her way; she was planning one step at a time. She did not know how—or where—she would live outside the convent; she had faith that the answer would come, and it did. It was the way she would approach the entire project, then and to this day.

She and her advisers made two decisions at once: that to work among the poor of India, she would need some training in basic nursing techniques; and also that she should dress in a sari, as the Indian women did.

On August 17, she left the convent for the city of Patna, to study nursing at a missionary hospital there. She packed her new habit, one that would become familiar to the whole world: three identical white saris trimmed in blue. They had been blessed for her by Father van Exem.

She spent barely four months in Patna. The medical missionary brothers there decided after only the most rudimentary training—perhaps with some urging from her—that she should go to work immediately and that whatever help she needed would come to her on the job.

She returned to Calcutta on December 9. The Sisters of Loreto had promised her a meager allowance for a while, and, armed with that, she went to live at the St. Joseph's Home for the Poor, run by the Little Sisters of the Poor. As she also would be from now on, they were vowed to poverty.

All nuns are vowed to poverty. In the convent, however, that vow is more formal than practical. An individual nun owns virtually nothing, but her order provides her with the basics of food, shelter, and clothing. Mother Teresa, on the other hand, was to have no order, no shelter, and, indeed, no food, except that which people would give to her.

Ten days after her return to Calcutta, on December 19, wearing her sari and a pair of rough sandals, she went out into the streets of Motijhil, one of Calcutta's worst slums. There, amid streams of raw sewage, she gathered together a few desperately poor children, sat them down under a tree, and began to teach them the rudiments of reading and writing—in the Bengali language—and of basic hygiene.

Chapter 12

Her "Second Self"

It is unclear when Mother Teresa knew that she would found a new order of nuns. Her journal from the early weeks in Motijhil suggests that the idea of the Missionaries of Charity had not yet occurred to her.

In any case, she realized her desire to form a new order soon enough when she got her first recruit, a young St. Mary's student named Subashini Das. "Subashini Das has joined the Little Society," she wrote exultantly in her journal on March 19, 1949.

Not long afterward, a second came, and then a third—serendipitously, a medical student, also from St. Mary's. The as yet unnamed "Little Society" was growing exponentially.

One other person joined Mother Teresa in spirit, though not geographically: a Belgian lay missionary named Jacqueline De Decker who would become perhaps the most important person in her life. For many years she has called De Decker her "second self."

De Decker and Mother Teresa had much in common. Somewhat younger than Mother Teresa, Jacqueline De Decker, too, had wanted in her adolescence to become a missionary in India, though without taking the veil. Instead, she had finished her education in Europe, earning a degree in sociology, before coming to India in 1947.

There she had taken to dressing Indian style, in saris and sandals, and, as much as possible, living as the Indians did. When she heard of a nun who did the same, she felt impelled to meet her.

The two felt an instant sympathy and made plans to work together, but before they could move their plans forward, De Decker was stricken with the first symptoms of a serious, painful spinal disorder that would eventually disable her. She returned to Europe for the first of many back operations, and her collaboration with Mother Teresa in the ensuing half-century has been conducted primarily via correspondence. Their extant letters provide the most extensive documentation of the early period of the Missionaries of Charity.

"26 May 1949—My Dear Miss De Decker...You will be glad to hear at present I have got three companions, great zealous workers. We have five different slums where we go for a few hours. What suffering, what want of God..." And, barely six months later, "19 November 1949—My dear Jacqueline... At present we are five, but please God more will join, and then we will be able to make a ring of Charity round Calcutta..."

Within another few months, Subashini Das would become Sister Agatha, and the Little Society would become Mother Teresa's own mission.

FROM THE BEGINNING, MOTHER TERESA HAS VISITED THE HOMES OF THE DESTITUTE AND THE DYING;

HERE SHE PRAYS FOR VICTIMS OF A RIOT.

Chapter 13

A New
Order

If the Missionaries of Charity

order was still only embryonic, its

future shape was clear from the

outset. Mother Teresa's new order

of nuns would serve the poor. In

order to do so, they would live in

the same poverty as those they

HAVING NOTHING, MOTHER TERESA AND THE MISSIONARIES HAVE NEVERTHELESS ALWAYS
"FOUND" WHAT THEY NEEDED FOR THEIR WORK; HERE THEY DISTRIBUTE RICE AND BLANKETS
ON CHRISTMAS EVE IN CALCUTTA.

served. They would accept no government grants but take only what people gave them. Each sister

would own three saris, one pair of rough sandals, and virtually nothing else.

"This is the only way we will be in a position to share the sufferings of the poor," said

Mother Teresa. "Strict poverty is our only safeguard. We do not want to happen to us what hap-

pened to other religious orders...that started out serving the poor and...ended up serving the rich."

But the poor would need material help as well. How were the sisters to provide that help if

they had nothing?

AT FIRST, MOTHER TERESA HAD TO BEG FOR FOOD AND SUPPLIES ON THE STREETS AND
DOOR-TO-DOOR; BUT OVER TIME, PEOPLE BEGAN TO COME TO HER WITH GIFTS.

FIFTY YEARS AFTER MOTHER TERESA LEFT THE SISTERS OF LORETO TO BE A LONE MISSIONARY
OF CHARITY, HER ORDER HAS GROWN TO INCLUDE MORE THAN FOUR THOUSAND NUNS AROUND
THE WORLD, MOST OF THEM BORN LONG AFTER THE ORDER WAS FOUNDED. THEY CONTINUE THE
WORK SHE FIRST BEGAN, FEEDING AND CLOTHING THE POOR, NURTURING THE ORPHANED,
CARING FOR LEPERS, AND MINISTERING TO THE DYING. HERE SHE LISTENS TO A SECOND
GENERATION OF U.S. MISSIONARY NUNS RENEWING THEIR VOWS.

The answer to that question goes to the heart of Mother Teresa's mission: she believed that as God had ordered her to found the order, God would provide the means to accomplish its ends. And to this day, she believes that miraculous is not too big a word for what she and her sisters have received.

Others have ascribed miracles to her, but Mother Teresa herself says only that the miracles are God's. Examples of God's generosity are plentiful. One day early on in her order's mission, the Missionaries of Charity awoke one morning to find they had nothing to feed to the children. Shortly after daybreak, a truck arrived; the Calcutta schools had closed for the day, and the truck was bringing her all the food the schools would have given out.

From the very beginning individuals made donations, as did the church. "One day," Mother Teresa says, relating one such event, "while I was walking in the streets of Calcutta, a priest came up to me, asking me to give a contribution for a collection for promoting some worthy project. That morning I had left the house with all the money I had, five rupees, which amounted to about thirty cents. During the day, I had spent four on food for the poor. I had only one rupee to live on the next day.... Trusting in God, I gave my last rupee to that priest.... The next evening a person whom I didn't know came to my shack. He gave me an envelope and said, 'This is for your work.' I opened the envelope and found fifty rupees."

Father van Exem put an advertisement in a Calcutta paper and contributions began to arrive. Late in December 1949—barely a year after she had left the convent—a parish priest gave

MOTHER TERESA AT WORK IN ONE OF THE MANY MISSIONARY OF CHARITIES HOMES FOR LEPERS IN INDIA.

A CATHOLIC ORDER, THE MISSIONARIES OF CHARITY IS NONETHELESS ECUMENICAL IN ITS
WORK. THE NUNS BURY THE DYING THEY HAVE NURSED ACCORDING TO THE RITES OF EACH
INDIVIDUAL'S RELIGION, AND THEY OBSERVE LOCAL HOLIDAYS ALONG WITH THOSE OF THE
CHURCH. HERE A GROUP OF YOUNG NUNS HELP CHILDREN LIGHT SPARKLERS FOR DIWALI,
INDIA'S FESTIVAL OF LIGHTS.

THOUGH HER DAILY SCHEDULE INCLUDES WORK ENOUGH FOR TWO PEOPLE, MOTHER TERESA
CAN SUSPEND EVERYTHING ELSE TO HELP WHEN DISASTER STRIKES. HERE SHE AIDS IN
CYCLONE RELIEF IN VIJAYAWADA, INDIA.

her money to rent two rooms to house her school. The Missionaries of Charity had grown to ten women teaching twenty-one children.

The order became formalized in January 1950. With the help of advisers, including Father van Exem, Mother Teresa drew up the rules—or Constitutions—for the order. The Missionaries of Charity would differentiate themselves from other orders by vowing themselves not only to poverty, chastity, and obedience, but to a life of service to the "poorest of the poor."

Yet the sisters were not to be not social workers. "Above all," Mother Teresa told an interviewer, "[a typical day] consists of prayer. Contrary to what people think, we are not sisters who are engaged in an active life....Prayer...is fundamental for us. We always pray, whether it be walking down the street, during our work, or wherever. If we're not continually united with God, it would be impossible to make the sacrifices that are required for living among those who have been forsaken." In their Constitutions, it is written, "We must leave every project for the future in the hands of an Omnipotent God, because yesterday has gone by, tomorrow is not yet here, and today we have only to know, love, and serve Jesus."

The same month she wrote the Constitutions, Mother Teresa opened a dispensary to provide medicine for the people of Motijhil, and in February, she and her sisters moved into a home of their own, in Calcutta's Creek Lane.

In October, word came from Rome: the Missionaries of Charity had been approved by the pope. Mother Teresa was the head of a recognized order of nuns.

From that point on, the order mushroomed with astonishing speed, limited only by Mother Teresa's capacity to imagine new outlets for the collective energy of the Missionaries. Church law forbade her from opening missions outside of India until ten years had passed, but for the time being, India was a large enough field of endeavor.

In 1952, the Missionaries began a new enterprise. In Mother Teresa's words, "One day, while I was leaving our house, I came across a man lying on the sidewalk who was at the brink of death....I went to get help at a nearby hospital, but...when I returned after a few minutes, he was already dead. He breathed his last breath in the dust on the street."

"It was a shame. I almost felt guilty....Then the idea occurred to me of creating a home where these dying people could finish out their lives, where someone would help them."

Thus they founded their first home for the dying. As previously, when they needed something, they received it: they were given the use of an abandoned temple to Kali, the Hindu goddess of death. It became the house called *Kalighat*, or *Nirmal Hriday*, the Home for the Dying. Now at least some of those who lived on the streets of Calcutta would no longer have to die there. There would be a place where the homeless could die in at least a minimal degree of comfort and dignity.

"PRAYER IS FUNDAMENTAL TO US," SAYS MOTHER TERESA OF HER ORDER. "IF WE'RE NOT

CONTINUALLY UNITED WITH GOD, IT WOULD BE IMPOSSIBLE TO MAKE THE SACRIFICES THAT

ARE REQUIRED FOR LIVING AMONG THOSE WHO HAVE BEEN FORSAKEN." THE NUNS RISE AT 4:30 IN THE

MORNING FOR AN HOUR-AND-A-HALF OF PRAYER TOGETHER BEFORE GOING

ABOUT THEIR DAILY WORK.

CALCUTTA MISSIONARIES OF CHARITY GATHER TO CHANT "HAPPY BIRTHDAY" TO THEIR FOUNDER ON HER EIGHTIETH BIRTHDAY.

A year later, in February 1953, the order had outgrown the Creek Lane house. The Missionaries of Charity now consisted of Mother Teresa and twenty-six other nuns. Archbishop Perier advanced them the money for the purchase of the building now called the Motherhouse, at 54A Lower Circular Road in Calcutta. The property consisted of one three-story building and several smaller ones, moving Mother Teresa to exclaim, "What shall we do with such a large house?"

In no time it was full, bustling with new Sisters of Charity engaged in ever more diverse works. The visits to the areas where the poor lived remained the core of their mission, but soon they were training young women in various skills, seeking out the tubercular and the leprous to provide them with medicine, and, as always, caring for children. In 1954 they opened the children's home called Shishu Bhan.

Later, Mother Teresa would muse, "Communist workers in Calcutta [wanted] to know the secret of the sisters' influence....Why [did] poor people listen to the sisters and not to the Communists, who promise them comfort on earth? There is no secret; the sisters preach and practice love."

New nuns were joining the order in large numbers, but laypeople wanted to share in the Missionaries' work as well. Between 1949 and 1954 thousands did so, in one way or another.

In 1954, the same year she opened the children's home, Mother Teresa decided to formalize a lay organization that would work with the Missionaries. Mother Teresa had been in India for most of the years that the great Mohandas Gandhi had led the emerging nation toward freedom. He was assassinated in 1948, the year she left the convent. Borrowing his terminology, she took to calling the lay adjuncts of the Missionaries "Co-Workers," and in 1954 the Co-Workers were formally organized into a worldwide association of women, men, and children. Jacqueline de Decker would become its director.

In the mid-1950s, Mother Teresa and her Missionaries began the work that would bring them to the public eye for the first time: they began to help victims of leprosy. In 1965 the Indian government gave the Missionaries of Charity a thirty–four–acre plot of land near the city of Asansol, the very place to which Mother Teresa had been exiled while she waited for permission to begin her mission. Here the Missionaries built a leper colony that they called *Shanti Nagar*, the Town of Peace.

Part IV
Citizen of the World
(1965-1979)

Chapter 14

The Woman Inside the Sari

WHO WAS THIS WOMAN, THIS DYNAMO,

THIS FORCE OF NATURE—OR OF GOD—

WHOM A VISION IN A RAILROAD TRAIN

HAD UNLEASHED UPON AN UNSUSPECT-

ING WORLD?

IN 1960, MOTHER TERESA WAS

FIFTY YEARS OLD, A FORMER TEACHING

BY THE 1990S MOTHER TERESA HAD BECOME THE MOST COSMOPOLITAN NUN IN HISTORY. IN
1995, SHE RETURNED TO THE LAND WHERE SHE WAS BORN—THE FORMER YUGOSLAVIA—TO
VISIT WAR-STRICKEN BOSNIA.

nun who had done one extraordinary thing: at eighteen she traveled halfway around the world, alone,

to follow a call and then nothing else for another eighteen years. The sisters of her own novitiate

describe her as a "nice," "simple" girl. Father Julien Henry, a Calcutta priest who knew her when

she first arrived in India, said of her many years later, "God has used this woman…because she is

completely subservient to Him."

It is an evaluation to which Mother Teresa wholeheartedly subscribes. Over and over since the first dawning of her worldwide celebrity she has said that she herself is nothing, merely an instrument of a divine will.

Certainly, her story can be read that way. Yet like an optical illusion, her story looks very different when viewed from a different perspective. It is that of a woman of formidable energy, creativity, intellect, and even, perhaps, ambition, who under different circumstances could have become anything from a poet to a politician—and who might well have become a Nobel laureate in any of those occupations.

A poet? Mother Teresa has written poems, many of them, but all you have to read is her business card. She had it made up when a businessman she was soliciting for donations told her she should have one. "Jesus is happy to come with us," her business card says, "as the truth to be told, as the life to be lived, as the light to be lit, as the love to be loved, as the joy to be given, as the peace to be spread."

A politician? She is one. In fact, she's a very successful one, lobbying around the world more and more for her constituents.

Worth noting in this context is the fact that although those close to her, particularly Catholics, tend to accept her at her face-value, strangers and non-Catholics often describe someone rather different. "One shrewd cookie," said a U.S. pacifist who spent an afternoon at an international conference with Mother Teresa.

There is another contradictory facet to this complex figure: a professed nun, who does everything she does "for Jesus," she nevertheless does not proselytize. Although some critics have attacked her for upholding Catholic doctrine—she is reputed to have told at least one journalist that her children's home is "how we fight contraception and abortion"—strict Catholics have complained that she flies in the face of that doctrine by evenhandedly encouraging all religious expression among those she serves. She says, "I 'convert' you to be a better Hindu, a better Catholic, a better Muslim or Jain or Buddhist. I would like to help you to find God. When you find Him, it is up to you to do what you want with Him."

IN ENGLAND TO RECEIVE ONE OF HER MANY AWARDS AND PRIZES.

The truth may be the same one George Bernard Shaw saw in the story of Joan of Arc, who also ascribed her extraordinary leadership—and the form it took—to commands from God. Like Joan, Mother Teresa came from a time and place that offered few models for female leadership. Shaw believed that the French saint actually heard her own inner voice as the voices of saints because she could not consciously believe that she herself was the author of her daring plans and insights.

Perhaps it is divine Providence that has for fifty years now dropped everything the Missionaries of Charity need into their collective laps. But perhaps, just perhaps, divine Providence has had a helping hand from the more-than-ordinary drive and persuasiveness that are as much a part of Mother Teresa as is her love of God.

Chapter 15

BEYOND INDIA

IN 1960 ANOTHER TURNING POINT CAME

FOR MOTHER TERESA AND THE

MISSIONARIES: SHE LEFT INDIA FOR THE

FIRST TIME SINCE HER ARRIVAL THERE

MORE THAN THIRTY YEARS BEFORE.

ALTHOUGH THE ORDER WAS STILL

CONFINED BY CHURCH LAW TO THE

borders of India, Mother Teresa was not, and that year she began the crisscrossing of the globe that has since become so frequent. She came to the United States for a religious conference. On her way back to Calcutta, she stopped in Rome to speak with Pope John XXIII about a particular request: since the Missionaries were part of no other order of nuns, she wanted them to be directly under the Vatican in the church hierarchy. As usual, the reply was not immediate.

Meanwhile, of course, she had work in Calcutta. She was now operating children's homes, the Home for the Dying, the leper colony, and schools in Asansol and other areas in India. For her work there, the Indian government gave her its *Padmashree* (Magnificent Lotus) Award in September 1962, the first time the award had ever been given to someone not born in India.

The same year, in recognition of her work there, the Philippine government bestowed its *Ramon Magsaysay* Award on her. That award came with a substantial cash honorarium of 50,000 rupees; it arrived just as Mother Teresa had nearly despaired of finding funds to open a lepers' treatment center and colony in Agra (where the Taj Mahal is located).

The neat timing of the Magsaysay Award and the 50,000 rupees has served ever since as one of Mother Teresa's myriad pieces of evidence of divine support for the Missionaries of Charity. Truth to tell, however, there have been few moments in the last fifty years in which Mother Teresa has not been planning some major expansion of her work, one that requires a large infusion of funds. Any substantial sum that arrives, therefore, always comes just in the nick of time to rescue such a project, and unless one perceives the very existence of the awards as providential, miraculous seems a strong adjective for their arrival.

Meanwhile, Mother Teresa was trying to effect yet another innovation: she had come to believe that there were aspects of the Missionaries of Charity's work to which men were better suited. Their charges in the children's home, for example, were growing, and there were now adolescent boys among them who were increasingly unsuited for life among a group of nuns. The nuns had always had help from parish priests and from laymen, of course, but more and more Mother Teresa felt the need for an organization of priests that would parallel her order. The Missionaries of Charity needed a brother organization.

AS IS TRUE OF MOST NOBEL PRIZE LAUREATES, MOTHER TERESA WAS WELL-KNOWN AROUND

THE WORLD LONG BEFORE SHE RECEIVED THE NOBEL PRIZE; SHE HAD ALREADY BEEN ON THE

COVER OF TIME MAGAZINE. BUT WHEN SHE WON THE NOBEL, PHOTOGRAPHERS BEGAN TO FOL-

LOW HER AROUND AS THEY WOULD A FILM STAR.

She tried to organize one, but there were roadblocks. She herself could not create an order for men—church law forbade a woman to head such an order—nor was there a group of men at hand, like the young women from St. Mary's a decade earlier, with whom to start an order.

As it has so many times in her career, help arrived, this time in the form of a young Jesuit priest named Brother Andrew. Almost before he knew it, he was the head of a fledgling order of priests called the Brothers of Charity, approved by the archbishop of Calcutta in 1963.

The Brothers expanded the Missionaries' work in more ways than Mother Teresa had imagined. The Calcutta railroad station, for example, teemed with homeless people, many of them youths. Early on, the Brothers took to rescuing those boys and young men.

Late in 1964 a new present came for Mother Teresa. On a trip to India, Pope Paul VI came to meet with her in Bombay. After the meeting, he turned over to her—or, rather, to the Missionaries of Charity—a luxury car that had been sent to him by U.S. Catholics.

Following that meeting, in 1965, she received two long-awaited responses from the pope: he placed the Missionaries of Charity directly under the control of the papacy and finally authorized Mother Teresa to expand the order outside India. Wasting no time, she personally opened a Missionaries of Charity house in Cocorote, Venezuela, in July of that year.

From that point on, new houses sprung up like mushrooms in every part of the globe, most of them opened by Mother Teresa herself. In her mid-fifties, she was, if anything, more vigorous than ever.

Chapter 16

The Last
Family Ties

terms with the pope himself and would soon be meeting with heads of state around the world. In 1968, in what must have seemed to her at the time as a kind of crowning glory, Pope Paul VI called her to Rome to invite her to found a Missionaries of Charity congregation there.

But during that same period—for perhaps the only time since 1946—Mother Teresa had an ambition, or at least a desire, in which her order played no part. After years of silence, she had received letters from her mother and sister in Tirana, but only one a year. Of all the eastern European nations, Albania, under Enver Hoxha, was probably the most repressed. Drone's and Agatha's letters were almost certainly read by agents of the state before they reached Mother Teresa. Though they said little, it was clear they were not happy, and in any case, Drone was nearing eighty. Mother Teresa had decided to get them out of Albania, if she could.

By then she was well known around the world. She persuaded France's foreign minister, Maurice Couve, to write to the Hoxha government on her behalf and plead for Drone and Agatha to be allowed to visit her.

After an interminable wait, Couve received a reply. It said, "Mrs. Drone Bojaxhiu and Miss Agatha Bojaxhiu are not in a physical condition that would allow them to travel abroad."

No appeal was possible. Two decades later, after the collapse of the communist states of eastern Europe, Mother Teresa would visit Albania herself, but far too late to see her beloved mother. Drone died there in 1972 at the age of eighty-three; her youngest daughter Agatha survived her by little more than a year, dying in 1973. She was only sixty years old.

THREE YEARS AFTER POPE PAUL VI ASKED MOTHER TERESA TO FOUND A MISSIONARIES
OF CHARITY HOUSE IN ROME, HE CALLED HER BACK TO RECEIVE THE FIRST JOHN XXIII PEACE PRIZE,
NAMED FOR THE ECUMENICAL, PEACE-LOVING POPE WHOSE BRIEF TENURE (1958–1963) TOUCHED
THE HEART OF THE WORLD.

"S■METHING BEAUTIFU

FOR GOD"

MOTHER TERESA HAS BEEN CALLED A

LIVING SAINT BY MANY, AND SHE HER-

SELF DESCRIBES THE WAY HER ORDER

RECEIVES FUNDING TO ACCOMPLISH ITS

MISSION AS MIRACULOUS. SO FAR,

THOUGH, ONLY ONE ACTUAL MIRACLE

HAS BEEN ASCRIBED TO HER, BY A

respected British film journalist who captured it on film and broadcast it on television for all the world to see.

In 1969, at the very point that the Missionaries of Charity were going global, the usually sardonic Malcolm Muggeridge went to Calcutta with a film crew to see Mother Teresa for himself. He later wrote that at the Kalighat Home for the Dying the love that pervaded the rooms was "luminous, like the haloes artists have seen and made visible round the heads of the saints."

He attempted to set up a film shoot, but the home was "dimly lit by small windows high up in the walls, and [the camera operator] was adamant that filming was quite impossible there."

They decided to try anyway, and the results astonished Muggeridge: the room "was bathed in a particularly beautiful, soft light....I am convinced that the technically unaccountable light is, in fact, the Kindly Light [of the hymn of the same name]."

Muggeridge brought his film back to England, broadcast it in a documentary about Mother Teresa, and then wrote a book based on the documentary, both of them titled *Something Beautiful for God*. In the book, he stated explicitly that he believed he had been a witness to a genuine miracle.

The documentary and the book made Muggeridge more famous than he had ever been before—and they made their subject a household name. Indeed, *Something Beautiful for God* stands in a sense as the threshold between the life of a simple, if innovative, Calcutta nun and the woman whose face is known across the globe.

There are many who believe that Mother Teresa is a genuine saint and that she will be canonized by the Church as early as possible, and that canonization requires not only what we think of as a saintly life but actual evidence of an actual miracle. It may be that Muggeridge's documentary will go down in history as the first such evidence on camera.

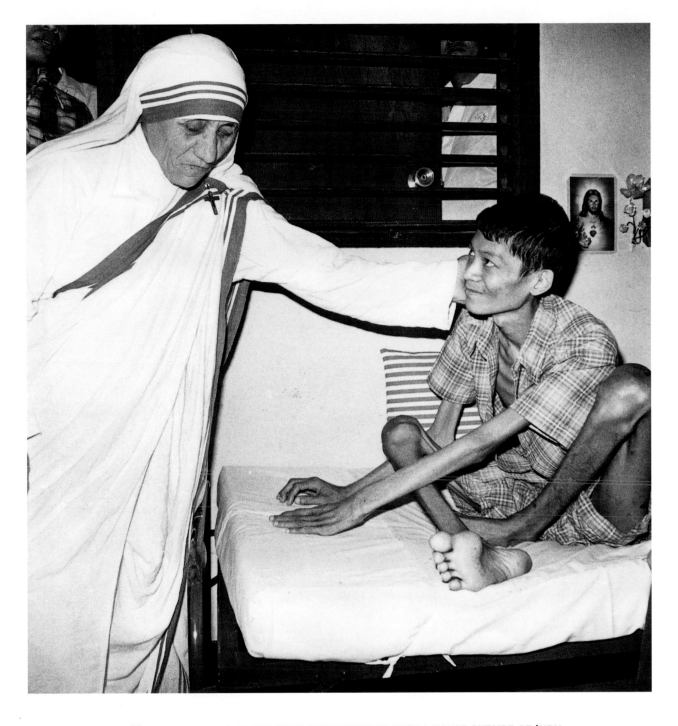

WITHIN FIVE YEARS OF RECEIVING PERMISSION TO OPEN A HOUSE OUTSIDE OF INDIA,
MOTHER TERESA HAD OPENED MISSIONARIES OF CHARITY IN SOUTH AMERICA, EUROPE,
AFRICA, AND AUSTRALIA. HERE SHE VISITS A YOUNG POLIO VICTIM AT HER
HOME FOR THE DESTITUTE IN MANILA.

THE WORLD
WIDE MISSION

Of all the ever-growing Missionaries

of Charity's broad efforts, it was

those with and for children that

most touched the world's heart-

strings—and also that generated

the most controversy.

MOTHER TERESA RECEIVES A BLESSING FROM POPE JOHN PAUL II.

The nuns took in every abandoned or unwanted child who came their way. Some were dying, but many were destined to remain in the Sisters' homes for their entire childhoods. If a home was filled to overflowing, Mother Teresa would simply open another. By the early 1970s, there was more than one in many of the major cities of India. Some held twenty children, some as many as two hundred; most were urban, but some were attached to lepers' colonies. A journalist described one as "full of cheerful children at play, [with the] sound of laughter resound[ing] constantly."

Mother Teresa rejected the thought that there might be no room for a child. She loved to repeat an old Calcutta joke on the subject: "Mother Teresa does not practice family planning," it goes, "every day she has more and more children." After initially begging for food in the streets of Calcutta for them, she became involved in worldwide efforts to place the children in foster homes.

But to joke about "family planning" was to acknowledge, at least implicitly, the criticisms that were leveled against her on that account. In a part of the world considered by many to be suffering more from overpopulation than any other single ill, her outspoken opposition to contraception and abortion—she is among those who refer to abortion as a "war" against children—has been the target of more attacks than any other aspect of her work.

For Mother Teresa, it is both a simple matter of Catholic doctrine as well as something more personal. Children, she repeats endlessly, are a "gift from God" and cannot be unwanted.

Despite the controversy, however, the honors continued to flow in, along with—and far more important to her—ever-increasing resources for the order. By the beginning of the 1970s, Mother Teresa's schedule looked like that of a jet-setter or a head of state. In 1970 alone, she opened Missionaries of Charity houses in Jordan, Australia, and in London; the last was particularly dear to her heart, a novitiate where Missionaries of Charities novices could train for the life they would lead as nuns.

CONSIDERED A LIVING SAINT BY MANY, MOTHER TERESA INSPIRES DEVOTION WHEREVER SHE TRAVELS.

She traveled not only to open new houses, but also to receive the many accolades for her care of the children. Early in 1971, Pope Paul VI honored Mother Teresa by awarding her the first Pope John XXIII Peace Prize. Later that year she returned to the United States, opening houses in Boston, New York, and Washington. Still later she personally opened a new house in Northern Ireland.

In 1972 she suffered one of her worst setbacks when she took four sisters to Northern Ireland to open a Missionaries of Charity House in Belfast. In the face of the wrenching struggles there between Catholics and Protestants, she wanted to create an institution that would heal. But Belfast found no room for a foreign Catholic mission. Some months later she and the four nuns returned to Calcutta.

The following year the government of India presented her with the Jawaharlal Nehru Award for International Understanding. In 1973 she met with Emperor Haile Selassie of Ethiopia to discuss opening a mission there, and she met with Prince Philip of England in London to receive yet another award.

"Prince Philip was charming," she said later. "He had kind words to say about our [order]. During the meal he enquired about our work. . . . They served only one course; I suppose it was out of consideration for me and my work among the poor."

There are those who have criticized her, indeed, for meeting with and accepting cooperation and sometimes financial aid for her order from heads of state without regard to their government's stances or even their records on human rights. She has responded, "If you are working for peace, then that lessens war. But I won't mix in politics. . . . If I got stuck in politics, I would stop loving—because I would have to stand by one, not by all."

There are more, of course, who accept her uncritically and even reverently. In 1975 *Time* magazine ran a lead article on "Living Saints," with Mother Teresa's picture on the cover, and in 1977, Cambridge University awarded her an honorary doctorate. But the greatest worldly honor was still to come.

THE NOBEL PRIZE

IN 1979, ONE OF THE GREATEST HONORS
THIS WORLD HAS TO OFFER WAS
BESTOWED UPON MOTHER TERESA: THE
NOBEL PRIZE FOR PEACE.
GOVERNMENTS AND THE CHURCH HAD
LONG SINCE HONORED MOTHER TERESA
AND HER WORK; NOW SHE RECEIVED THE

MOTHER TERESA ACCEPTS THE NOBEL PRIZE FROM JOHN SANNES, CHAIRMAN OF THE
NORWEGIAN NOBEL COMMITTEE, IN OSLO, DECEMBER 10, 1979.

highest accolade of the most prestigious nongovernmental organization in the world, the Nobel Committee.

She also received the cash award that accompanied the prize: a not insignificant $250,000. The money, of course, would go toward her work, as did every contribution, large and small.

But the prestige was hers. Conferring the award on her in Oslo, in the presence of the King of Norway and other international luminaries, Professor John Sannes, Chair of the Nobel Committee, said, "There could be no better way of describing the intentions that have motivated the decision of the…Committee than the comment of the President of the World Bank [former U.S. Secretary of Defense] Robert S. MacNamara when he declared, 'Mother Teresa deserves Nobel's Peace Prize because she promotes peace in the most fundamental manner by her confirmation of the inviolability of human dignity.'"

As if echoing his words, Mother Teresa then accepted the prize, speaking to the glittery audience of the gritty details of the lives of the poor in Calcutta. She then asked them to cancel the usual post-ceremony dinner and give the money to feed those who had nothing to eat.

ON ONE OF HER MANY VISITS TO THE UNITED STATES, MOTHER TERESA RECEIVES COMMUNION

IN THE BASILICA OF THE ASSUMPTION, IN BALTIMORE—THE OLDEST CATHOLIC CHURCH

IN THE COUNTRY.

PART V
AUTUMN
(1979–1997)

ILLNESS AND  SURGERY

THE NOBEL PRIZE WAS THE CROWNING

GLORY OF MOTHER TERESA'S CAREER IN

MORE WAYS THAN ONE, FOR IT WAS NOT

LONG AFTER RECEIVING IT THAT SERIOUS

HEALTH PROBLEMS BEGAN TO ENCROACH

ON HER SCHEDULE.

VISITING A MISSIONARIES OF CHARITY ORPHANAGE IN PORT-AU-PRINCE, HAITI.

If anything, her traveling was increasing—in 1980 and 1981, she was in Haiti, Ethiopia, and the United States again (this time to open a house in inner Washington, D.C.). But the unremitting work took its toll on the aging nun. Mother Teresa had turned seventy; she had been in India for more than fifty years. In 1983 heart problems escalated into a need for constant medical supervision, and she had to have a pacemaker installed.

It was the first of many heart surgeries. As time wore on, she also began to suffer increasingly from osteoporosis, the decrease in bone mass that makes many older people fragile.

Fragile, however, was not a word Mother Teresa would allow to be applied to her. For the next fifteen years, except when actually in the hospital, she would continue her work just as she had done for the last fifty.

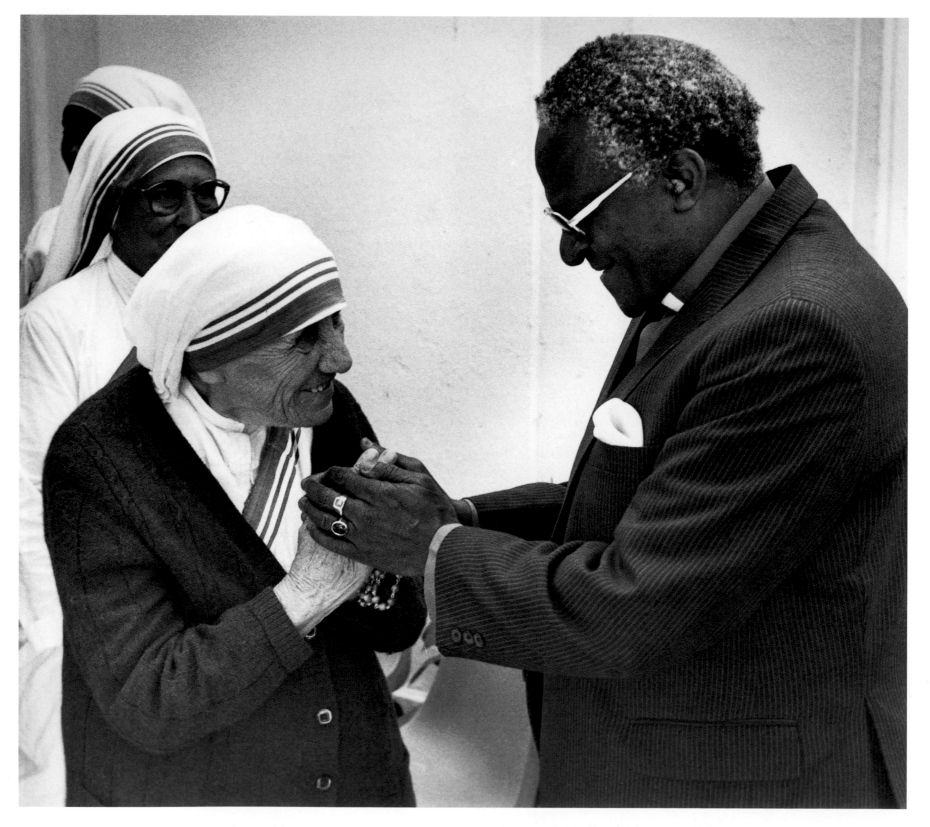

Two Nobel laureates: Mother Teresa and Archbishop Desmond Tutu, in Cape Town, 1988.

IN FRONT OF THE WHITE HOUSE WITH PRESIDENT RONALD REAGAN AND FIRST LADY
NANCY REAGAN, DURING A 1981 VISIT.

As evidence that the work continued virtually unabated, one need only note that she has been hospitalized not only in her own Calcutta but also in California (twice), in other U.S. cities, and in Tijuana, Mexico.

When she left the hospital in Mexico, she went to Rome to recuperate—and, of course, to tend to Missionaries of Charity business there. While there, she was visited by Princess Diana of England. Also that same year, in India, Queen Elizabeth II conferred on her the prestigious British Order of Merit; thus, Mother Teresa has met individually both with Queen Elizabeth II and Prince Philip and with Prince Charles and Princess Diana.

In 1985, as a tribute to Mother Teresa's undiminished energy, U.S. President Ronald Reagan awarded her the Presidential Medal of Freedom during one of her now-frequent trips to the United States.

The Indomitable Mother Teresa

On a bone-chilling morning in February 1981 I met Mother Teresa in a tiny convent in Kathmandu. She sat with her bare feet on the icy stone floor, giving off the appearance of a simple and humble nun, but it took only seconds to feel the power of this indomitable woman's persona. After a brief exchange in which she extolled the virtues of the poor, proclaiming the blessing that many children bring to families and denouncing efforts to stem population growth, she got right down to business. With one of her local followers, she set an agenda for accomplishing the task ahead: to expand her projects for the poor and dying in Nepal. After receiving a briefing about the royal personalities it would be her task to charm, and the possible obstacles that lay ahead in a country in which proselytizing is against the law, she laid out a strategy to be followed. In a warm and friendly manner, she thanked me for coming and invited me to visit her center on the shore of the Bagmati River. She had a busy day ahead, one in which she would have to call upon all her abilitiies to charm and persuade, but it was clear to me that her expertise in promotion and public relations guaranteed that in the end she would get what she wanted.

—Virginia Olsen Baron

Chapter 21

MOTHER TERESA
ON DEATH ROW

IN 1987 THE MISSIONARIES OF CHARITY

CONSISTED OF THREE THOUSAND NUNS IN

THREE HUNDRED FIFTY HOUSES IN EIGHTY

NATIONS. IN ADDITION, THE BROTHERS AND

THE CO-WORKERS, ACCORDING TO MOTHER

TERESA, NOW NUMBERED AN ASTONISHING

FOUR HUNDRED THOUSAND.

That year, Mother Teresa visited the United States, opening still another house in California, where, among her other activities, she visited the condemned men on San Quentin's Death Row.

One of the inmates, Michael Wayne Hunter, wrote with a fierce eloquence about his encounter with her:

I heard the guard...call: 'Don't go into your cells and lock up. Mother Teresa stayed to see you guys, too.' So I jogged up to the front in gym shorts and a tattered basketball shirt with the arms ripped out, and on the other side of the security screen was this tiny woman who looked one hundred years old. Yes, it was Mother Teresa.

You have to understand that, basically, I'm a dead man. I don't have to observe any sort of social convention; and as a result, I can break all the rules, say what I want. But one look at this Nobel Prize winner, this woman so many people view as a living saint, and I was speechless.

Incredible vitality and warmth came from her wizened, piercing eyes. She smiled at me, blessed a religious medal, and handed it to me. I wouldn't have walked voluntarily to the front of the tier to see the Warden, the Governor, the President, or the Pope. I could not care less about them. But standing before this woman, all I could say was, 'Thank you, Mother Teresa.' Then I stepped back to let another dead man come forward to receive his medal.

Some years later, when another of the men she visited that day was scheduled for execution, Mother Teresa personally called California's governor Pete Wilson to ask for clemency for him.

NOT CONTENT WITH FEEDING THE HUNGRY, CLOTHING THE NAKED, SHELTERING THE HOMELESS
AND MINISTERING TO LEPERS, MOTHER TERESA HAS ALSO—AT LEAST IN THE UNITED STATES—
PRAYED WITH AND FOR THE CONDEMNED.

Chapter 22

THE FIRST RETIREMENT

MOTHER TERESA'S ILLNESS SLOWED

HER DOWN VERY LITTLE. NEARING

EIGHTY YEARS OLD, SHE NEVERTHELESS

TRAVELED TO MOSCOW IN FEBRUARY

1988, TO EXPLORE THE POSSIBILITIES

OF OPENING A HOUSE THERE. IN THOSE

ALL AROUND THE WORLD, THE NUN FROM THE WAR-TORN BALKANS HAS COME TO SYMBOLIZE PEACE
AND LOVE; HERE SHE RELEASES A WHITE DOVE PRESENTED TO HER IN TORONTO IN 1982.

early days of Glasnost and Perestroika it could still be difficult to gain entrance to behind the iron

curtain, but she won the coveted permission.

There certainly were houses virtually everywhere else. By 1990, more than three thousand

nuns belonged to the Missionaries of Charity, with centers in twenty-five countries. But Mother

Teresa's heart continued to give her trouble, and in March 1990 she resigned as Superior General of the order. For the first time in forty years, the nuns of her congregation disobeyed her: they voted her out of retirement. Giving in gracefully, she returned to her post in September.

The next year, she came as close as she ever had to meddling in politics. On 2 January 1991, as the clock ticked in the countdown toward the Gulf War between U.S. and U.N. forces and Iraq, she sent a personal letter to both Saddam Hussein and President George Bush, pleading with them to find a peaceful solution to the crisis.

"Dear President George Bush and President Saddam Hussein," she wrote. "I come to you with tears in my eyes and God's love in my heart to plead to you for the poor and those who will become poor if the war we all dread and fear happens. I beg you with my whole heart to work for, to labour for God's peace and to be reconciled with one another. . . . In the short term there may be winners and losers in this war that we all dread, but that never can nor ever will justify the suffering, pain, and loss of life which your weapons will cause." She signed it, "God bless you, M. Teresa."

Her peacekeeping effort failed, but Hussein's government invited her there to help the orphaned and the disabled after the war.

By now she was constantly having to fit one medical crisis after another into her undiminished schedule. That same year, 1991, after the fall of the communist government of Albania, she visited her ancestors' country for the first time, meeting with the widow of Enver Hoxha, the dictator who had virtually imprisoned her mother and sister. And later that year, when an earthquake killed thousands in Bangladesh, she was there as quickly as transportation could be arranged, though she was just out of the hospital.

During another trip to the United States, she was hospitalized in Los Angeles and had to undergo more heart surgery. Yet even under her faltering direction, the Missionaries of Charity continued to grow. By 1992—the same year yet another heart attack hospitalized her in Mexico—the order had added another five hundred nuns, for a total of thirty-five hundred in four hundred forty-five houses in ninety-five countries.

According to Mother Teresa's records, the order was treating one hundred fifty thousand lepers a year in India alone, not only in the centers but via an innovative mobile unit.

"I BEG YOU WITH MY WHOLE HEART TO WORK FOR ... GOD'S PEACE," MOTHER TERESA WROTE TO
PRESIDENTS GEORGE BUSH AND SADDAM HUSSEIN ON THE EVE OF THE GULF WAR. NOT LONG
AFTERWARD, BUSH RECEIVED HER IN THE WHITE HOUSE, AS HAD HIS PREDECESSOR,
RONALD REAGAN.

WELL OVER EIGHTY YEARS OLD AND BESET BY HEART DISEASE AND OTHER AILMENTS, THE INDOMITABLE NUN

WAS STILL TRAVELING THE WORLD AND RUNNING THE FOUR THOUSAND–STRONG MISSIONARIES OF CHARITY. HERE

SHE SPEAKS AT A U.S. PRESS CONFERENCE IN 1995.

But in 1993, she underwent still more heart surgery—she was home in Calcutta at the time. And the next year, she was brushed for the first time by scandal, when American journalist Christopher Hitchens broadcast a fiercely critical documentary about her in England. Hitchens accused her of consorting with and taking money from some of the worst dictators and criminals on the planet, citing photographs of her with Michèle Duvalier, wife of Haitian dictator "Baby Doc" Duvalier, Hoxha's widow, and convicted financier Charles Keating, among others. He also took her to task for conforming to Church doctrine by opposing birth control and abortion in one of the most overpopulated countries in the world.

The accusations were not so much false as beside the point. Except for her refusal of ongoing government support, Mother Teresa has never picked nor chosen who can facilitate her mission, accepting all donors with equal gratitude. On behalf of the Missionaries of Charity, she has accepted alms from anyone who offered them, from those almost as poor as the people she serves to the heads of state of virtually every nation on the face of the earth. Beggars have come to her door and pleaded with her to accept the few rupees they would otherwise have for rice, and schoolchildren around the world have sent her their saved pennies. To her, all aid is part of the miracle that keeps the Missionaries of Charity at work.

PASSING ON THE MISSION

AFTER HER FIRST HEART SURGERY, MOTHER TERESA TOLD A JOURNALIST, "I WORK FOR GOD. HE'LL TELL ME WHEN IT'S TIME TO STOP."

SHE FINALLY RECEIVED THAT MESSAGE IN 1997, SEVERAL MONTHS BEFORE HER EIGHTY-SEVENTH BIRTHDAY.

MOTHER TERESA VISITED THE GIFT OF LOVE AIDS HOSPICE DURING A TWO-DAY VISIT TO
SAN FRANCISCO IN 1989.

She had been ill for much of the preceding autumn. In November 1996, hospitalized again
with chest pains, the question had arisen as to what efforts would be made to save her life or resus-
citate her. Her answer was, "Let me die like the poor that I serve."

Her physicians, however, were reluctant to let their world-renowned patient die under their
care and begged and pleaded with her to let them take stronger measures. Finally, late in November,
she agreed to still another angiography, which was performed by the same doctor who had operat-
ed on her in 1991 and 1993. In addition to the cardiac problems, however, Mother Teresa was also
suffering from severe osteoporosis, which made it doubly difficult for her to function normally. She

remained bedridden, at home in the Motherhouse or in the hospital, through the turn of the year.

It was fifty years since she had founded the order. Finally she recognized that it was time to step down. In February 1997, God told her it was time to stop.

Filling her sandals, however, was not to be an easy task. The order now numbered more than four thousand nuns operating five-hundred-seventeen houses and projects around the globe. The most logical choice for her successor might have been Sister Agnes, the one-time St. Mary's school-girl Subashini Das who, fifty years before, had become the first Sister of Charity. But Sister Agnes, now sixty-six and in failing health herself, felt unable to take on the formidable task.

Early in February, the order's electoral college converged on the Motherhouse in Calcutta for what was expected to be a week-long retreat to choose its next head. The retreat lasted over a month as the nuns tried to articulate the criteria for their leadership. Pope John Paul II urged them to select a woman of "deep spirituality," yet surely it had been as much Mother Teresa's charisma as her religious ardor that had forged the Missionaries' success.

For weeks, the world watched as the nuns debated. Newspapers from Calcutta to New York issued bulletin after bulletin on the progress of the selection. Finally, on March 13, 1997, the order announced a decision: the new head of the Missionaries of Charity would be the little-known Sister Nirmala, at sixty-three the chief of the order's contemplative wing.

Born Nirmala Joshi into a high-caste Indian family, Sister Nirmala had been inspired to convert to Catholicism by the order's efforts on behalf of the poor and despised. Now she would direct those efforts. "I am in dreamland," she told the press after the choice was announced. But she added, "I don't know how far I will be able to carry out the work successfully. I will try, and with the blessings of Mother and God, I will be able to carry it out." And from the balcony of the Motherhouse, Mother Teresa told the world, "Now I am happy. Pray so she can continue God's work."

Only a few months later, on September 5, Mother Teresa passed away. One of the twentieth century's most beloved figures, Mother Teresa left a lasting legacy of love and faith that will continue to inspire people the world over.

"NOW I AM HAPPY." MOTHER TERESA INTRODUCES SISTER NIRMALA, HER INDIAN-BORN SUCCESSOR AND THE FORMER

HEAD OF THE MISSIONARIES OF CHARITY'S CONTEMPLATIVE WING TO THE WORLD FROM THE BALCONY OF THE

MOTHERHOUSE IN CALCUTTA ON MARCH 14, 1997. MOTHER TERESA FINALLY HANDED OVER TO YOUNGER HANDS

THE MISSION SHE FOUNDED OVER FIFTY YEARS EARLIER.

BIBLIOGRAPHY

Allegri, Renzo. *Teresa of the Poor*. Ann Arbor, Mich.: Charis Books, 1996.

Burns, John F. "Followers Struggle to Fill Mother Teresa's Sandals," *The New York Times*, March 9, 1997.

Chawla, Navin. *Mother Teresa: The Authorized Biography*. Rockport, Mass.: Element Books, 1992.

Clucas, Joan Graff. *Mother Teresa*. New York: Chelsea House, 1988.

Hitchens, Christopher. *The Missionary Position: Mother Teresa in Theory and Practice*. London/New York: Verso, 1995.

————. "Minority Report," *The Nation*, April 13, 1992.

Le Joly, Edward. *Servant of Love: Mother Teresa and the Missionaries of Charity*. San Francisco: Harper & Row, 1977.

Various. "Independence of India and Pakistan," *Compton's Interactive Encyclopedia*, 1995.

————. "Let Me Die Like Those I Serve: Mother Teresa," *The Times of India*, November 27, 1996.

————. "Living Saint Steps Down," *New York Daily News*, March 14, 1997.

————. "Mother Agrees for Angiography," *The Times of India*, November 27, 1996.

————. "Mother Bedridden," *The Times of India*, January 13, 1997.

————. "Mother Teresa's Successor Will Be Chosen on Feb. 2," *The Times of India*, January 15, 1997.

Weinberg, Bill, and Dorie Wilsnack. "War At the Crossroads: An Historical Guide Through the Balkan Labyrinth," War Resisters League, Balkan War Resource Group, 1995.

PHOTOGRAPHY CREDITS

Agence France Presse/Corbis-Bettmann: p. 117

AP/Wide World Photos: pp. 11, 18, 23, 26, 30, 37, 43, 45, 46, 51, 62, 67, 69, 72, 76, 87, 91, 94, 95, 97, 101, 104, 115

Archive Photos: p. 64;
Camera Press: p. 10;
Express Newspapers: p. 56;
Reuters: ©Joe Giza: p. 66;
©Kamal Kishore: p. 107;
©Mallace: p. 25;
Popperfoto: pp. 1, 77, 79;
©Brian Snyder: p. 112

Art Resource: Archives Larousse-Giraudon: p. 34

Catholic New Service: ©Michael Alexander: p. 58

FPG International: ©Greg Gilman: p. 22

©Robert Fried: endpapers, pp. 6–7, 8, 12–13, 14, 24, 28–29, 52–53, 74–75, 98–99

Leo de Wys Inc. N.Y.: pp. 55, 114;
©Jon Hicks: p. 57

©Rick Maloof: pp. 2, 36, 47, 84, 105, 108

Reuters/Corbis-Bettmann: pp. 19, 68, 102

REX USA LTD.: pp. 21, 92;
©John Shelley: p. 100

UPI/Corbis-Bettmann: pp. 9, 15, 31, 33, 63, 65, 71, 82, 86, 89, 90, 103, 109, 111

©Sonam Zoksang: p. 39, 44, 48, 49, 50, 54, 60, 80

Map Illustrations: Oliver Yourke

INDEX